This Journal Belongs To

Made in the USA
Monee, IL
19 April 2022

95009721R00063